KS1
4–6
Years

Master Maths at Home

Geometry and Shape

Scan the QR code to help your child's learning at home.

 |

mastermathsathome.com

How to use this book

Maths — No Problem! created **Master Maths at Home** to help children develop fluency in the subject and a rich understanding of core concepts.

Key features of the Master Maths at Home books include:

- Carefully designed lessons that provide structure, but also allow flexibility in how they're used. For example, some children may want to write numbers, while others might want to trace.

- Speech bubbles containing content designed to spark diverse conversations, with many discussion points that don't have obvious 'right' or 'wrong' answers.

- Rich illustrations that will guide children to a discussion of shapes and units of measurement, allowing them to make connections to the wider world around them.

- Exercises that allow a flexible approach and can be adapted to suit any child's cognitive or functional ability.

- Clearly laid-out pages that encourage children to practise a range of higher-order skills.

- A community of friendly and relatable characters who introduce each lesson and come along as your child progresses through the series.

You can see more guidance on how to use these books at **mastermathsathome.com**.

We're excited to share all the ways you can learn maths!

Copyright © 2022 Maths — No Problem!

Maths — No Problem!
mastermathsathome.com
www.mathsnoproblem.com
hello@mathsnoproblem.com

First published in Great Britain in 2022 by
Dorling Kindersley Limited
One Embassy Gardens, 8 Viaduct Gardens, London SW11 7BW
A Penguin Random House Company

The authorised representative in the EEA is Dorling Kindersley
Verlag GmbH. Amulfstr. 124, 80636 Munich, Germany

10 9 8 7 6 5 4 3 2
003–327066 –Jan/22

A CIP catalogue record for this book is available from the British Library.

ISBN: 978-0-24153-907-1
Printed and bound in the UK

For the curious
www.dk.com

This book was made with Forest Stewardship Council™ certified paper - one small step in DK's commitment to a sustainable future. For more information go to www.dk.com/our-green-pledge

Acknowledgements
The publisher would like to thank the authors and consultants Andy Psarianos, Judy Hornigold, Adam Gifford and Dr Anne Hermanson.

The Castledown typeface has been used with permission from the Colophon Foundry.

Contents

Ruby   Elliott   Amira   Charles   Lulu   Sam   Oak   Holly   Ravi   Emma   Jacob   Hannah

Ordinal numbers

Starter

In what order did the children get on the school bus?

Example

| 1st first | 2nd second | 3rd third | 4th fourth |

I got on the bus before 🙂. I was the 2nd to get on.

I was the 4th to get on the bus. I got on the bus after Ravi.

4

1 Use **1st, 2nd, 3rd, 4th, before** or **after** to fill in the blanks.

(a) The [plane] was the [_____] to land at the airport.

(b) The [plane] landed [_____] the [plane].

(c) The [plane] was the [_____] to land at the airport.

(d) The [plane] landed [_____] the [plane].

2 In what order did the planes land?
Use **first, second, third** and **fourth** to fill in the blanks.

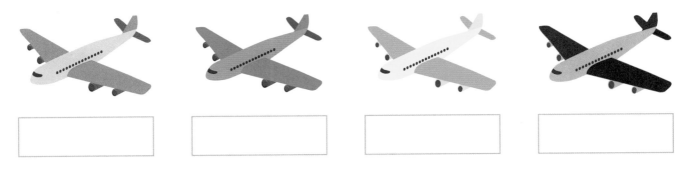

[_____] [_____] [_____] [_____]

Describing positions in queues

Starter

Ten cars are in a queue to start a race.

Can you name their positions in the queue?

Example

| | 2nd second | | 4th fourth | | 6th sixth | | 8th eighth | | 10th tenth |

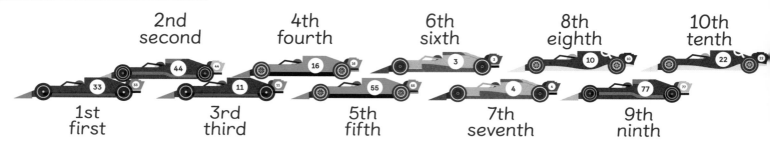

| | 1st first | | 3rd third | | 5th fifth | | 7th seventh | | 9th ninth |

Car 33 is in front of all the other cars. It is starting in first place.

I hope car 3 wins. There are 5 cars in front of it. It is starting in sixth place.

The numbers on the cars do not tell us their position in the queue.

6

Use the pictures in the Starter and Example sections to complete the table.
Fill in the blanks.

1

1st	first	[car 33]
	second	[car 44]
3rd		[car 11]
4th		[car 16]
	fifth	[car 55]
6th		[car 3]
	seventh	[car 4]
8th		[car 10]
	ninth	[car 77]
	tenth	[car 22]

2   (a) [car 3] is [_____] in the queue.

   (b) The first car in the queue is [_____].

   (c) [car 11] is between cars [_____] and [_____].

   (d) The car before [car 77] is [_____].

   (e) The car after [car 55] is [_____].

Naming left and right positions

Starter

How can we describe the position of each object?

Example

The ball is first from the **left**.

The pencil case is fifth from the left.

The paint pot is second from the **right**.

The book is third from the right.

The book is in the **middle**.

I am starting from the left.

I am starting from the right.

The book is also third from the left.

1 Write the missing words.

(a) The general store is second from the ⬚ .

(b) The ⬚ is second from the right.

(c) The ⬚ is fourth from the left.

(d) The pizza restaurant is between the general store

and the ⬚ .

2 Follow these instructions to draw 5 items in the box.

⬚

(a) Draw a book in the middle of the box.

(b) Draw a teddy bear at the end of the box on the right.

(c) The first item on the left in the box is a pencil pot.

(d) Draw a doll between the pencil pot and the book.

(e) The ball is the fourth item from the left and the second item from the right.

Recognising 3D shapes

Starter

What shapes can you see?

Example

Pyramids and cuboids all have corners.

These are **pyramids**.

These are **cuboids**.

This shape is also called a cube. It is a special cuboid because all the sides are the same length.

These are **spheres**.

This is a **cylinder**.

1 Go on a shape hunt around your home.
Fill in the table with the objects that you find.

Shapes	Objects
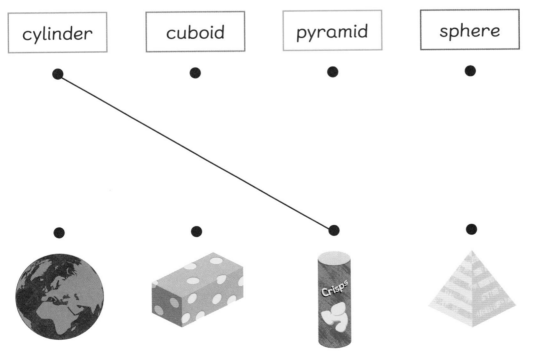	

2 Match each picture to a name.

cylinder	cuboid	pyramid	sphere

Recognising 2D shapes

Starter

What shapes can you see?

Example

These shapes are **triangles**.

These shapes are **rectangles**.

This shape is also called a square. It is a special rectangle. All of its sides are the same length.

These shapes are **circles**.

1 Go on a shape hunt around your home.
Fill in the table with the objects that you find.

Shapes	Objects

2 Describe a shape to someone in your family.
Can they guess which shape you are describing?
Take turns to describe different shapes.

3 (a) Colour all the triangles.   (b) Colour all the rectangles.

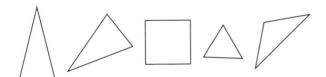   

(c) Colour all the squares.   (d) Colour all the circles.

Sorting shapes

Starter

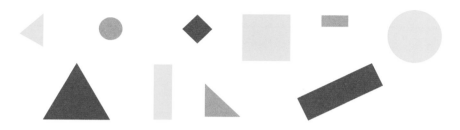

In how many ways can you sort these shapes?

Example

I sorted them by shape.

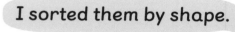

I sorted them by size.

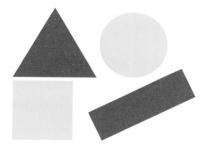

I sorted them by colour.

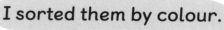

1 Circle the shapes that are the same shape as the first ones shown.

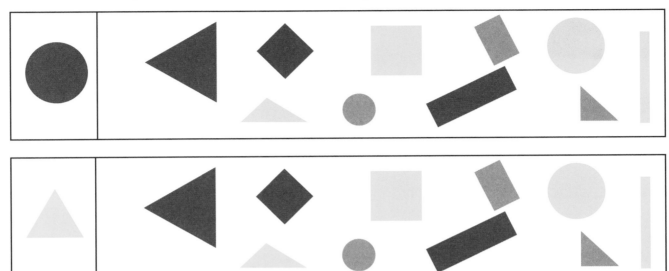

2 How are the shapes sorted?

(a)

These shapes are sorted by [   ].

(b)

These shapes are sorted by [   ].

(c)

These shapes are sorted by [   ].

Making repeating patterns

Starter

Can you describe this pattern?

Example

The shapes stay the same.

The colours change.

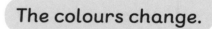

We can describe this pattern as orange star, blue star.

Only the size of the triangles change here.

1 Draw the shapes to continue these patterns.

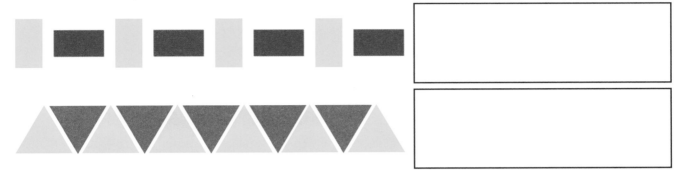

2 Make your own pattern and draw it here.

What stays the same? What changes?

3 Look at the shapes that repeat and circle one group.
Colour the shape that comes next in the pattern.

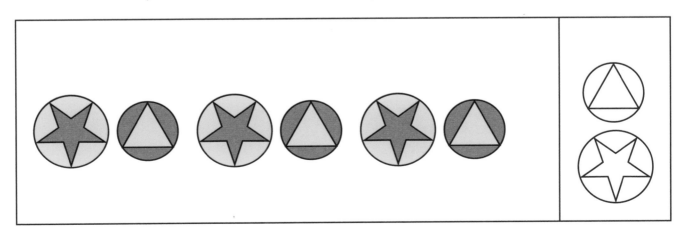

Making more repeating patterns

Starter

Can you describe this pattern?

Example

All the shapes are triangles, but they are not all the same size.

Some triangles are red, some are pink and some are blue.

The pattern is: large red triangle, small pink triangle, large blue triangle, small pink triangle.

This is called a repeating pattern.

18

1 Draw the missing shapes to complete the patterns.

(a)

(b)
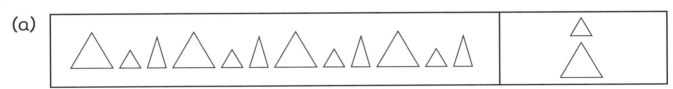

2 Colour the shapes to make a repeating pattern. Use 3 different colours. Circle the shape that comes next in the pattern.

(a)

(b)
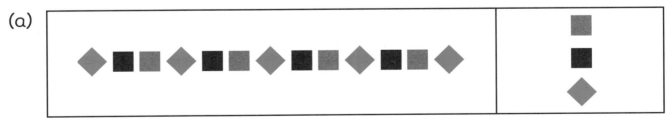

3 Circle the shape that comes next in the pattern.

(a)
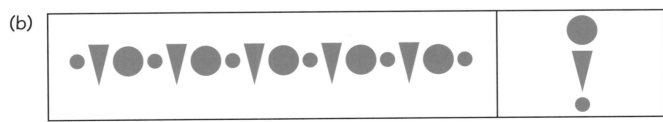

(b)

Describing positions: inside and outside

Starter

How can we describe where Ruby is?

Example

Ruby is **inside** the house.

Ruby is **outside** the house.

1 Find some things that are normally inside your home.
Draw some of them here.

2 Find some things that are normally outside your home.
Why do we keep those things outside?

3 Fill in the blanks using **inside** or **outside**.

Do you keep a car inside the house or outside the house?

(a) We keep milk [_____] the fridge.

(b) The dustbin stays [_____] the house.

(c) When it is sunny, Hannah likes to have a picnic [_____] .

Describing positions: far from and close to

Starter

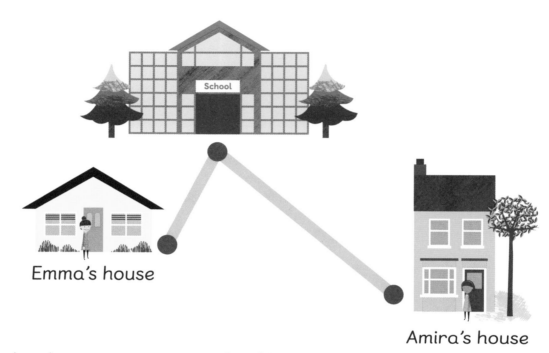

Who has the shorter journey to school?

Example

Emma's house is **close to** the school.

Amira's house is **far from** the school.

Emma has the shorter journey to school.

I live next door to the school.

I don't live close to my school.

22

1 Look at the picture and fill in the blanks with
far from or **close to**.

(a) Lulu is sitting [   ] Elliott.

(b) Charles is sitting [   ] Amira.

(c) Ruby is sitting [   ] Hannah.

2 Draw a dog close to the tree.
Draw a cat far from the tree.

Describing positions: on top of, underneath and between

Starter

How can we describe the position of Ruby's cat?

Example

Ruby's pillow is **underneath** her head.

Ruby is in her bed. She is **between** the mattress and the blanket.

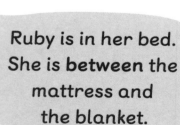

Ruby's cat is **on top of** the blanket.

24

1   Look at the picture. Fill in the blanks using **on top of**, **underneath** and **between**.

(a) Charles's dog is [   ] the table.

(b) The plates are [   ] the table.

(c) The blue plate is [   ] the hot dogs and the table.

2   Fill in the blanks using **on top of** and **underneath**.

(a) You spread butter [   ] toast.

(b) You sleep [   ] the mattress and [   ] the blanket.

3   Draw a book on top of a table and a crayon on top of the book.

Fill in the blanks using **on top of, underneath** or **between**.

(a) The book is [   ] the table and the crayon.

(b) The table is [   ] the book.

Describing positions: in front of and behind

Starter

How can we describe the position of the train?

Example

> The train is **in front of the** station.

behind

> The station is **behind the** train.

in front

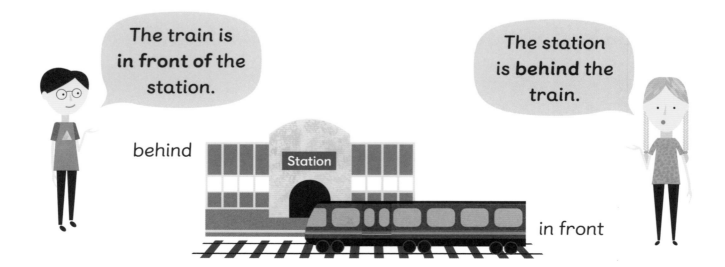

1

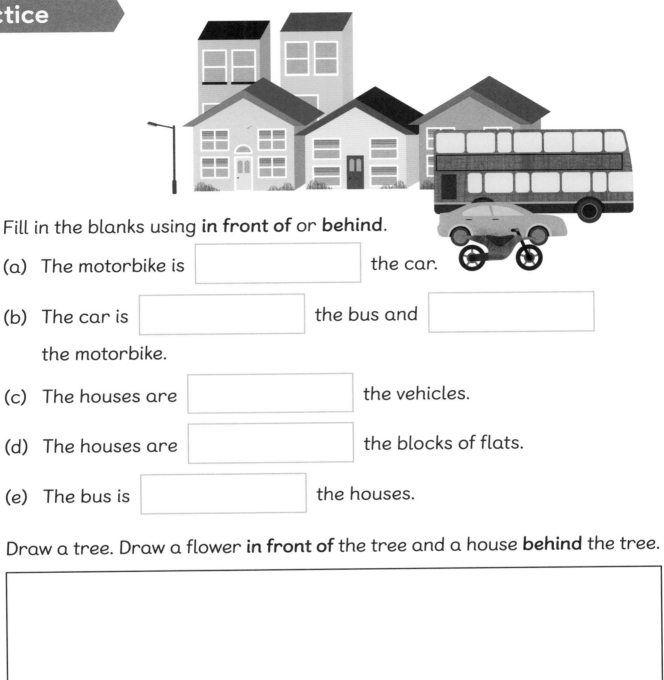

Fill in the blanks using **in front of** or **behind**.

(a) The motorbike is [_____] the car.

(b) The car is [_____] the bus and [_____] the motorbike.

(c) The houses are [_____] the vehicles.

(d) The houses are [_____] the blocks of flats.

(e) The bus is [_____] the houses.

2 Draw a tree. Draw a flower **in front of** the tree and a house **behind** the tree.

[   ]

3 Fill in the blanks using **in front of** and **behind**.

(a) Amira is [_____] Ravi.

(b) Sam is [_____] Ravi.

Describing positions: above, top, middle and bottom

Starter

How can we describe the positions of the items on the shelves?

Example

The  are on the **middle** shelf.

The 🎂 are on the **top** shelf.

The 🍩 are on the **bottom** shelf.

We can also say that the  are **above** the 🧁
and the 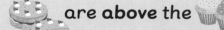 .

1

Fill in the blanks using **above**, **top**, **middle** and **bottom**.

(a) The strawberries are on the [   ] row.

(b) The apples and oranges are on the [   ] row.

They are [   ] all the other fruit.

(c) The bananas and pears are on the [   ] row.

2 (a) Draw a teddy bear on the middle shelf.

(b) Draw a car on the bottom shelf.

(c) Draw a ball on the top shelf.

Describing movements: up and down, over and under

Starter

What are Charles and Ravi doing?

Example

Charles is climbing up the stairs.

Ravi is walking down the stairs.

2

 is jumping **over** the hurdle.

 is crawling **under** the table.

Practice

1 Fill in the blanks using **up** and **down**.

(a)

The ball is moving [   ].

(b)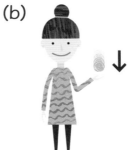

The ball is moving [   ].

2 Fill in the blanks using **over** and **under**.

(a) kicks the football [   ] the goal.

(b) The water flows [   ] the bridge.

Describing movements: forwards and backwards

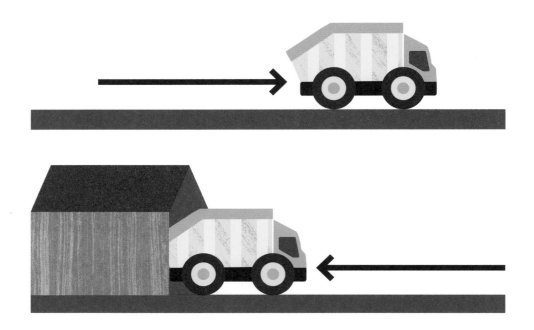

How can we describe the direction in which the truck is moving?

Example

When a vehicle moves backwards we say it is reversing.

I can count forwards and backwards. 1, 2, 3, 4, 5 ... 5, 4, 3, 2, 1.

The truck travels **forwards** and **backwards** .

Fill in the blanks using **forwards** or **backwards**.

1 (a)

(b)

2

 3, 4, 5, 6, 7

Lulu

8, 7, 6, 5, 4

Ravi

 15, 14, 13, 12

Jacob

33, 34, 35, 36

Emma

(a) Lulu is counting _____ .

(b) Ravi is counting _____ .

(c) Jacob is counting _____ .

(d) Emma is counting _____ .

Making turns: whole and half turns

By how much did Sam turn the roundabout?

Example

Sam turned the roundabout **1 half turn**.

It is facing the **opposite** direction.

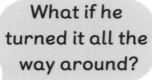

What if he turned it all the way around?

That is called a **whole turn**. It is facing in the **same** direction.

 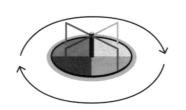  

1 Fill in the blanks using **whole** and **half**.

(a)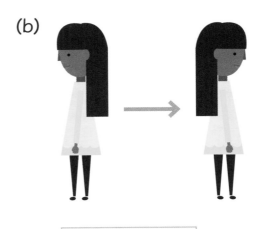

[   ] turn

(b)

[   ] turn

2 Fill in the blanks using **same** or **opposite**.

(a) When you make a whole turn you end up facing the

[   ] direction.

(b) When you make a half turn you end up facing the

[   ] direction.

(c) Charles makes three half turns. He ends up facing the

[   ] direction.

Making turns: quarter and three-quarter turns

Starter

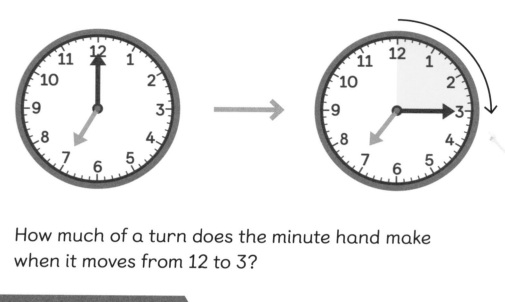

How much of a turn does the minute hand make when it moves from 12 to 3?

The minute hand is the long hand.

Example

When the minute hand moves from 12 to 3 it has moved **one quarter** of a turn.

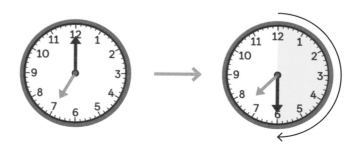

When the minute hand moves from 12 to 6 it has moved **one half** of a turn.

Now the minute hand has made a **three-quarter turn**.

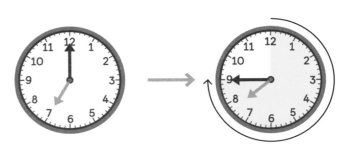

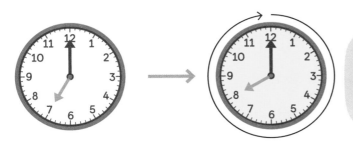

The minute hand has gone all the way around and it is back where it started. It has made a **whole turn**.

Practice

Fill in the blanks with **whole**, **quarter**, **half** or **three-quarter**.

1

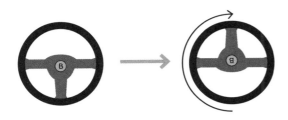

[   ] turn

2

[   ] turn

3

[   ] turn

4

[   ] turn

37

Making turns: clockwise and anticlockwise

Starter

In what direction does a clock turn?

Example

 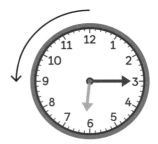

clockwise   anticlockwise

Clocks always turn in the same direction. We call that direction **clockwise**.

We call the opposite direction **anticlockwise**.

1 Fill in the blanks using **clockwise** and **anticlockwise**.

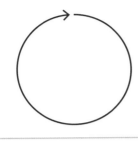

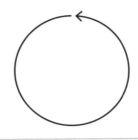

2 Draw arrows to show:

(a) a quarter turn clockwise

(b) a three-quarter turn anticlockwise

(c) a half turn anticlockwise

(d) a half turn clockwise

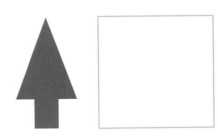

Review and challenge

1 Look at the pictures, then fill in the blanks.

[   ] is first in the race.

The last person is [   ].

[   ] is second.

2 Look at the pictures, then fill in the blanks.

potato   carrot   onion   mushroom   marrow

(a) The onion is [   ] from the left.

(b) The [image] is next to the [   ].

(c) The [   ] is between the potato and the onion.

3 Match.

 •

• sphere

 •

• cube

 •

• cylinder

 •

• pyramid

4 Trace the shape and match.

 •

• triangle

 •

• circle

 •

• rectangle

 •

• square

5 Complete the patterns.
Draw the shape that comes next in each pattern.

(a)

(b)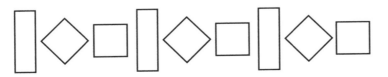

6 Draw the missing shape for each pattern.
Write the missing words.

Pattern A ☐ △ ☐ △ ☐ △ ☐

Pattern B ▯ ○ ⬭ ▯ ○ ⬭ ▯ ⬭

(a) The missing shape in Pattern A is a ☐ .

(b) The missing shape in Pattern B is a ☐ .

7 Draw a repeating pattern using a circle and a square.

8 Compare using **top**, **middle** and **bottom**.

(a) **C** is at the ☐ .

(b) **A** is at the ☐ .

(c) **B** is in the ☐ .

A
B
C

9 Describe using **on top of**, **in front of** and **above**.

(a) E E is [   ] D D .

(b) F F is [   ] D D .

(c) G G is [   ] D D .

10 Fill in the blanks using **inside** or **outside**.

(a) ⬤ is [   ] the box.

(b) ▭ is [   ] the box.

(c) ▲ is [   ] the box.

(d) ◼ is [   ] the box.

11 Fill in the blanks using **close to** and **far from**.

(a) England is [   ] Canada.

(b) England is [   ] Scotland.

12 Describe using **up** and **down**.

(a)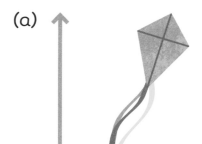

(b)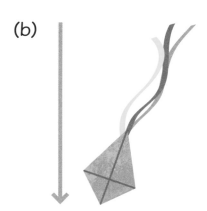

(a) The kite went [   ].

(b) The kite went [   ].

13 Fill in the blanks using **quarter**, **half**, **three-quarter** and **whole**.

(a)

The minute hand made

a [   ] turn.

(b)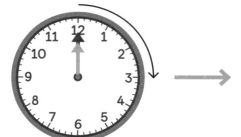

The minute hand made

a [   ] turn.

(c)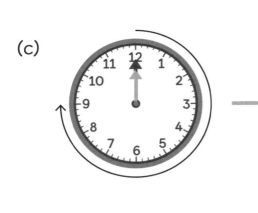

The minute hand made

a [ ] turn.

(d)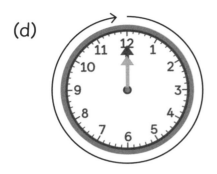

The minute hand made

a [ ] turn.

14

Charles makes a quarter turn anticlockwise. Ravi makes a half turn clockwise.

Will Ravi and Charles be facing in the same direction, or in opposite directions?

Tick to select the correct answer.

They will be facing the same direction [ ] .

They will be facing in opposite directions [ ] .

Answers

Page 5   **1 (a)** The blue plane was the 1st to land at the airport. **(b)** The red plane landed after the yellow plane. **(c)** The lilac plane was the 2nd to land at the airport. **(d)** The blue plane landed before the yellow plane. **2** second, fourth, third, first

Page 7   **1**

1st	first
2nd	second
3rd	third
4th	fourth
5th	fifth
6th	sixth
7th	seventh
8th	eighth
9th	ninth
10th	tenth

2 (a) Car 3 is sixth in the queue. **(b)** The first car in the queue is 33. **(c)** Car 11 is between cars 44 and 16. **(d)** The car before 77 is 10. **(e)** The car after 55 is 3.

Page 9   **1 (a)** The general store is second from the left. **(b)** The bakery is second from the right. **(c)** The bakery is fourth from the left. **(d)** The pizza restaurant is between the general store and the bakery.

2

Page 11   **1** Answers will vary.

2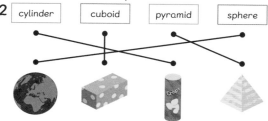

Page 13   **1** Answers will vary. **2** Answers will vary.

3 (a)

Page 15

2 (a) These shapes are sorted by colour. **(b)** These shapes are sorted by shape or number of sides. **(c)** These shapes are sorted by size.

Page 17   **1**

3 One group circled, for example:

Page 19 1 (a)  (b)

2 (a) One group coloured, for example:

(b) One group coloured, for example:

3 (a)  (b)

Page 21 1 Answers will vary. 2 Answers will vary. 3 (a) We keep milk inside the fridge. (b) The dustbin stays outside the house. (c) When it is sunny, Hannah likes to have a picnic outside.

Page 23 2 (a) Lulu is sitting far from Elliott. (b) Charles is sitting close to Amira. (c) Ruby is sitting far from Hannah.

3

Page 25 1 (a) Charles's dog is underneath the table. (b) The plates are on top of the table.
(c) The blue plate is between the hot dogs and the table.
2 (a) You spread butter on top of toast. (b) You sleep on top of the mattress and underneath the blanket.
3 (a) The book is between the table and the crayon. (b) The table is underneath the book.

Page 27 1 (a) The motorbike is in front of the car. (b) The car is in front of the bus and behind the motorbike. (c) The houses are behind the vehicles. (d) The houses are in front of the blocks of flats. (e) The bus is in front of the houses.

2 3 (a) Amira is in front of Ravi. (b) Sam is behind Ravi.

Page 29 1 (a) The strawberries are on the bottom row. (b) The apples and oranges are on the top row. They are above all the other fruit. (c) The bananas and pears are on the middle row.

Answers continued

2

Page 31 **1 (a)** The ball is moving up. **(b)** The ball is moving down. **2 (a)** Sam kicks the football over the goal. **(b)** The water flows under the bridge.

Page 33 **1 (a)** backwards **(b)** forwards **2 (a)** Lulu is counting forwards. **(b)** Ravi is counting backwards. **(c)** Jacob is counting backwards. **(d)** Emma is counting forwards.

Page 35 **1 (a)** whole turn **(b)** half turn **2 (a)** When you make a whole turn you end up facing the same direction. **(b)** When you make a half turn you end up facing the opposite direction. **(c)** He ends up facing the opposite direction.

Page 37 **1** half turn **2** quarter turn **3** three-quarter turn **4** whole turn

Page 39 **1** clockwise, anticlockwise **2 (a)** **(b)** **(c)** **(d)**

Page 40 **1 (a)** Sam is first in the race. The last person is Charles. Lulu is second. **2 (a)** The onion is 3rd (or third) from the left. **(b)** The marrow is next to the mushroom. **(c)** The carrot is between the potato and the onion.

Page 41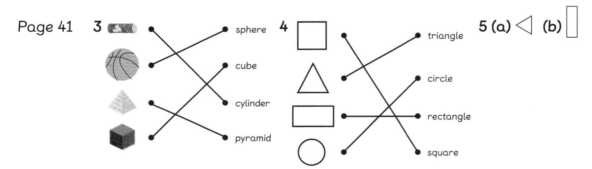

Page 42 **6 (a)** The missing shape in Pattern A is a square (or rectangle). **(b)** The missing shape in Pattern B is a circle. **7** Answers will vary. **8 (a)** C is at the bottom. **(b)** A is at the top. **(c)** B is in the middle.

Page 43 **9 (a)** E is above D. **(b)** F is on top of D. **(c)** G is in front of D. **10 (a)** The orange sphere is inside the box. **(b)** The green cuboid is outside the box. **(c)** The blue pyramid is outside the box. **(d)** The purple cube is inside the box. **11 (a)** England is far from Canada. **(b)** England is close to Scotland.

Page 44 **12 (a)** The kite went up. **(b)** The kite went down. **13 (a)** The minute hand made a half turn. **(b)** The minute hand made a quarter turn.

Page 45 **(c)** The minute hand made a three-quarter turn. **(d)** The minute hand made a whole turn. **14** They will be facing the same direction.